Everyone Eats

"Coloured Bedtime StoryBook"

By

Komar Rien Komar Cheh

Illustrated by

Chhoun Sambath

ILLUSTRATED & PUBLISHED
BY
E-KİTAP PROJESİ & CHEAPEST BOOKS

www.cheapestboooks.com

 www.facebook.com/EKitapProjesi

ISBN: 978-625-6308-91-6

Copyright, 2024 by e-Kitap Projesi

Istanbul

Categories: Non-fiction, Animals
Country of Origin: Cambodia
Cover: © Cheapest Books
License: CC-BY-4.0

For full terms of use and attribution, http://creativecommons.org/licenses/by/4.0/

Contributing: Chhoun Sambath

© **All rights reserved**.

Except for the conditions stated in the License, no part of this book shall be reproduced or transmitted in any form or by any means, electronic or mechanical, including photocopy, recording or by any information or retrieval system, without written permission form the publisher.

About the Book

Each animal likes different food. Let's find out what they all eat!

Everyone Eats

Komar Rien Komar Cheh
Chhoun Sambath

This is Cow.

Cow eats grass.

This is Chicken.

Chicken eats corn.

This is Horse.

Horse eats banana trees.

This is Elephant.

Elephant eats sugarcane.

This is Lion.

Lion eats raw meat.

They all live by eating food.

But Lion's food is different. Lion eats meat while the other animals eat plants.

End of the Story

www.ingramcontent.com/pod-product-compliance
Lightning Source LLC
LaVergne TN
LVHW070454080526
838202LV00035B/2833